TRADE CAREERS
ELECTRICIAN

by Joanne Mattern

pogo

Ideas for Parents and Teachers

Pogo Books let children practice reading informational text while introducing them to nonfiction features such as headings, labels, sidebars, maps, and diagrams, as well as a table of contents, glossary, and index.

Carefully leveled text with a strong photo match offers early fluent readers the support they need to succeed.

Before Reading

- "Walk" through the book and point out the various nonfiction features. Ask the student what purpose each feature serves.
- Look at the glossary together. Read and discuss the words.

Read the Book

- Have the child read the book independently.
- Invite him or her to list questions that arise from reading.

After Reading

- Discuss the child's questions. Talk about how he or she might find answers to those questions.
- Prompt the child to think more. Ask: Would you like to be an electrician? What do you like about this trade career?

Pogo Books are published by Jump!
5357 Penn Avenue South
Minneapolis, MN 55419
www.jumplibrary.com

Copyright © 2025 Jump! International copyright reserved in all countries. No part of this book may be reproduced in any form without written permission from the publisher.

Library of Congress Cataloging-in-Publication Data

Names: Mattern, Joanne, 1963- author.
Title: Electrician / by Joanne Mattern.
Description: Minneapolis, MN: Jump!, Inc., [2025]
Series: Trade careers | Includes index.
Audience: Ages 7-10
Identifiers: LCCN 2023057947 (print)
LCCN 2023057948 (ebook)
ISBN 9798892131582 (hardcover)
ISBN 9798892131599 (paperback)
ISBN 9798892131605 (ebook)
Subjects: LCSH: Electrical engineering—Vocational guidance—Juvenile literature. | Electricians—Juvenile literature.
Classification: LCC TK159 .M38 2025 (print)
LCC TK159 (ebook)
DDC 621.3023—dc23/eng/20240110
LC record available at https://lccn.loc.gov/2023057947
LC ebook record available at https://lccn.loc.gov/2023057948

Editor: Alyssa Sorenson
Designer: Anna Peterson
Content Consultant: Rob Zachariason, Electrical Technology Instructor, Minnesota State Community and Technical College

Photo Credits: Brian Hendricks/Shutterstock, cover (outlet); pokchu/Shutterstock, cover (wires); Volodymyr Krasyuk/Shutterstock, 1, 11 (voltage tester); DNY59/iStock, 3; Andrew Angelov/Shutterstock, 4; Wayne Via/Shutterstock, 5; Lisa F. Young/Dreamstime, 6-7; DonNichols/Getty, 8-9; MasterPhoto/Shutterstock, 10-11; Thomas Hecker/Shutterstock, 11 (pliers); Naruedom Yaempongsa/Shutterstock, 11 (drill); ariyan lukita/Shutterstock, 11 (wire strippers); photosync/Shutterstock, 11 (screwdriver); sturti/iStock, 12-13; Lisa F. Young/Dreamstime, 14; Grigvovan/Shutterstock, 15; FG Trade/iStock, 16-17; zstock/Shutterstock, 18; H. Mark Weidman Photography/Alamy, 19; Pixel-Shot/Shutterstock, 20-21; sockagphoto/Shutterstock, 23.

Printed in the United States of America at Corporate Graphics in North Mankato, Minnesota.

TABLE OF CONTENTS

CHAPTER 1
What Is an Electrician?........................4

CHAPTER 2
Learning the Trade............................14

CHAPTER 3
Where They Work..............................18

ACTIVITIES & TOOLS
Try This!....................................22
Glossary....................................23
Index.......................................24
To Learn More...............................24

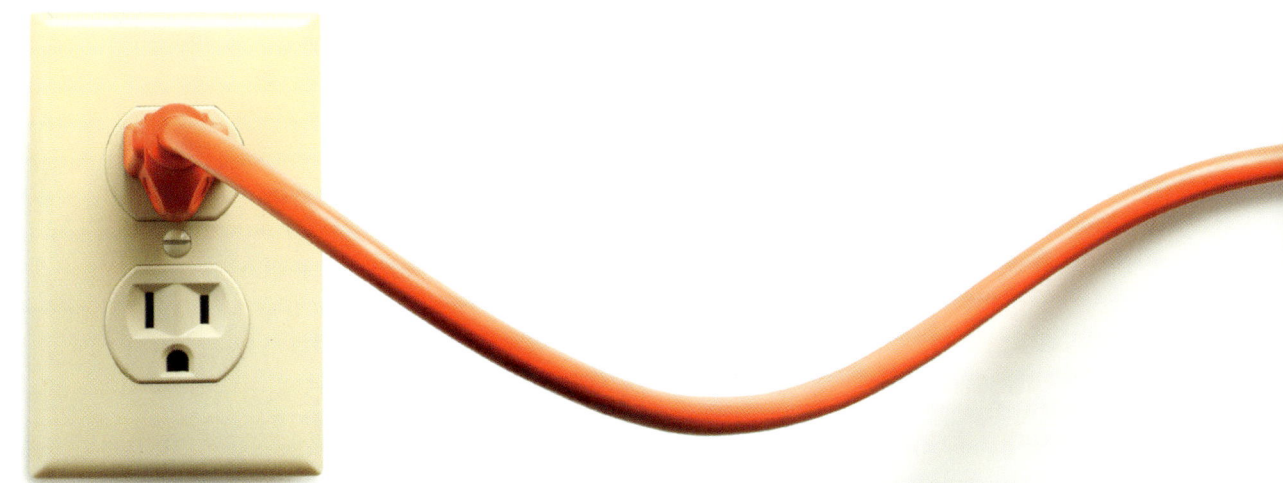

CHAPTER 1
WHAT IS AN ELECTRICIAN?

Electricians work with **electricity**. They test electrical equipment. They fix it. They put in lights. They connect power to buildings. They do a lot!

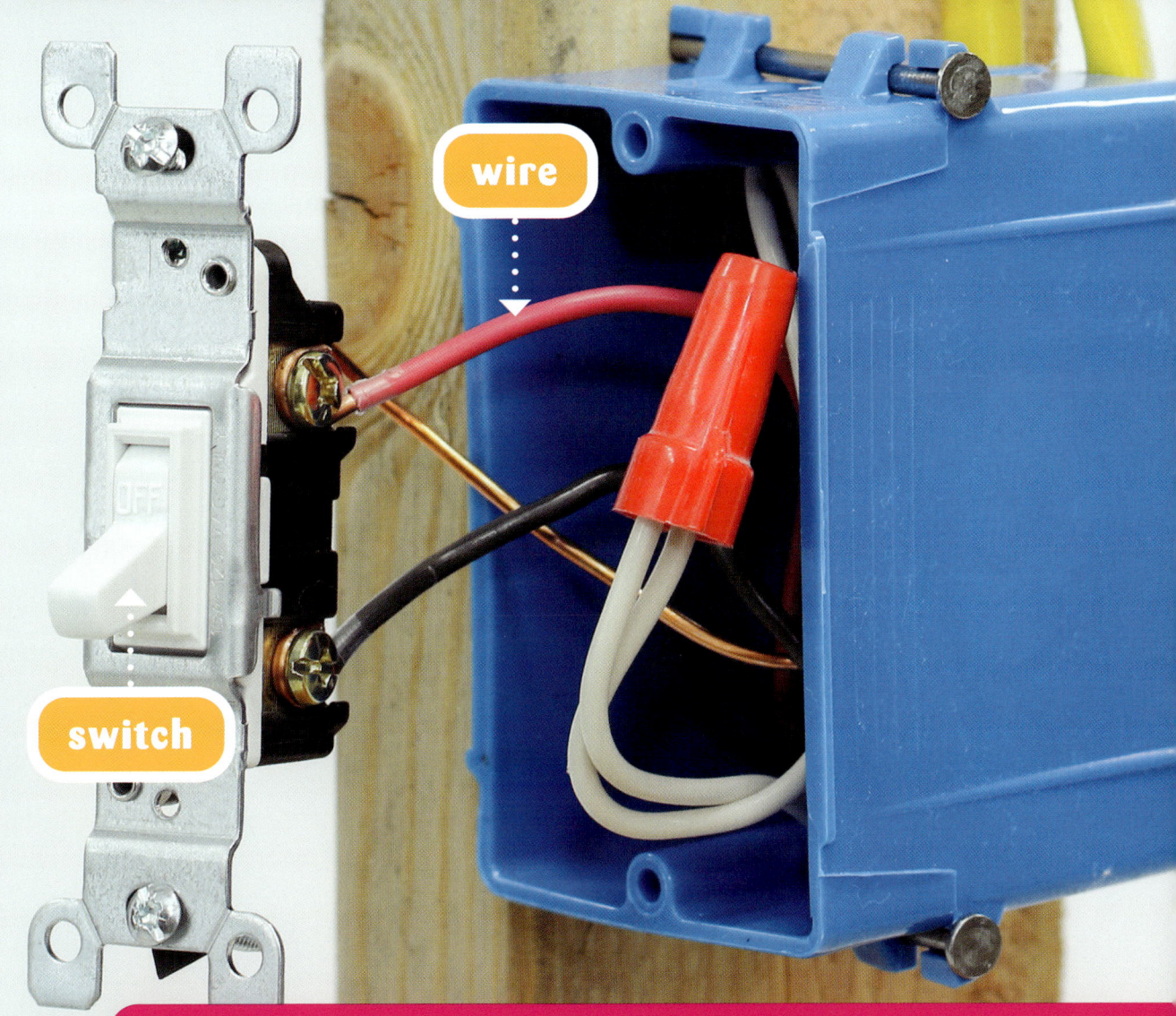

Wires carry electricity from power lines to buildings. Electricians connect wires to things like **switches**. Switches are connected to lights. People flip them on. Electricity goes to the lights. The lights turn on!

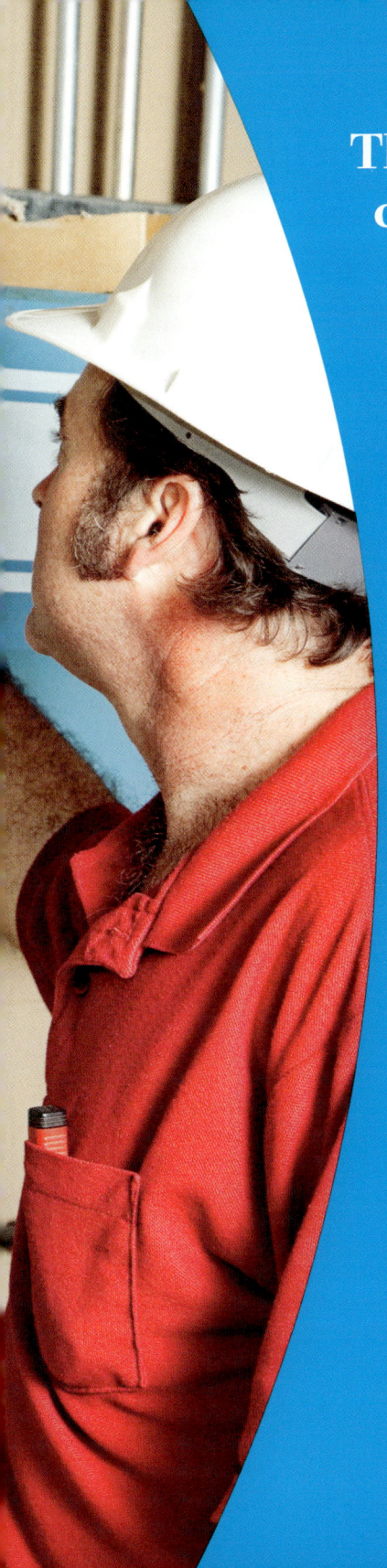

The power went out. An electrician comes. He looks at the electrical panel. Why? It brings electricity to the building. Something is wrong with it. The main **circuit breaker** has failed. The electrician puts in a new one. The power comes back on!

CHAPTER 1 | 7

A room needs a new **light fixture**. An electrician goes to the electrical panel. He finds the circuit breaker to the room. He flips the switch off. Why? This stops power from going to it.

He takes the old light off the ceiling. It is connected to wires. He takes a **voltage** tester. He touches it to the wires. He makes sure no electricity is going to the wires. That way, he will not get an **electric shock**.

CHAPTER 1

CHAPTER 1

After that, he connects the wires to a new light fixture. He flips the room's circuit breaker on. Then he flips the light switch. The new light works!

light fixture

TAKE A LOOK!

Electricians use many tools. What are some? Take a look!

pliers: cuts wires and holds wires and objects firmly

drill: makes holes and can be used to place or remove screws

voltage tester: tests if electricity is flowing

wire strippers: takes plastic coating off wires so electricians can work with them

screwdriver: places and removes screws

CHAPTER 1

Electricity can be dangerous. Electricians train for years. They learn how to work safely. They think before they act. They wear special clothing to keep them safe. For some projects, they wear **insulated** gloves. These protect their hands from electricity. Safety glasses protect their eyes from sparks.

DID YOU KNOW?

Electric shocks can hurt. They can cause burns. A person's **organs** might get hurt, too.

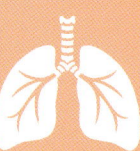

CHAPTER 1

CHAPTER 2
LEARNING THE TRADE

Do you want to be an electrician? You can study at a **vocational school**. You can become an **apprentice**, too. You will work with an experienced electrician. You will learn all about the **trade**. Apprenticeships often last four years.

apprentice

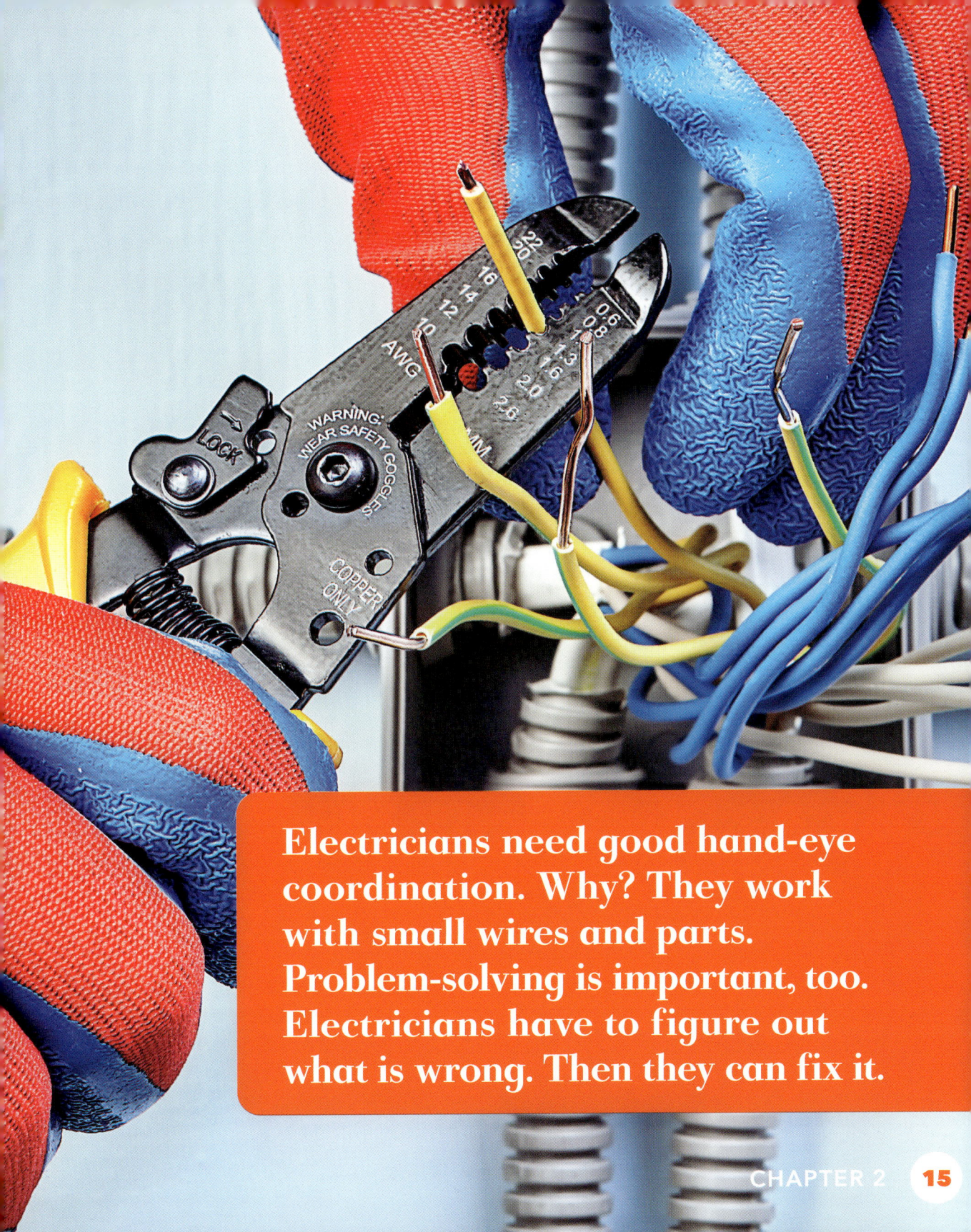

Electricians need good hand-eye coordination. Why? They work with small wires and parts. Problem-solving is important, too. Electricians have to figure out what is wrong. Then they can fix it.

In most states, electricians need a **license**. They must pass a test. A license shows they know how to work safely and correctly. People who pass this test are called journeyworkers.

DID YOU KNOW?

Journeyworkers can take another test. If they pass, they are a master electrician. They can start their own business!

CHAPTER 2

CHAPTER 3
WHERE THEY WORK

Some electricians work outside. Why? They put in **solar panels**. They work on streetlights.

solar panels

Others work inside. This might be in homes or factories. They might work at construction sites. They may put in wiring and electrical panels.

CHAPTER 3 19

We need electricians. Electrical systems need to be put in. They need to be fixed and kept working. Electricians have important jobs. Do you want to work with electricity?

DID YOU KNOW?

Electricians work on many jobs. Some last days or months. When the work is done, they move on to the next one.

CHAPTER 3 21

ACTIVITIES & TOOLS

TRY THIS!

LIGHT IT UP

Make a bulb light up! Ask an adult for help.

What You Need:
- battery
- copper wire
- small light bulb

① **Turn the light bulb sideways. Press the metal part of the bulb to the positive end of the battery.**

② **Hold the end of the wire to the negative side of the battery.**

③ **Take the other end of the wire. Press it to the bottom of the bulb. Does it light up?**

GLOSSARY

apprentice: Someone who learns a skill by working with an expert.

circuit breaker: A switch that protects a circuit from getting too much electric current.

electricity: Electrical power that is made in large plants and transported to different places through wires.

electric shock: The physical effect of an electric current touching the body.

insulated: Made of materials that stop electricity from passing through.

license: A document that gives someone permission to do certain work.

light fixture: Part of a light that attaches to the ceiling or wall and lets you insert one or more light bulbs.

organs: Parts of the body, such as the kidneys or heart, that serve a specific purpose.

solar panels: Panels that take the sun's rays and turn them into energy.

switches: Devices that stop or start the flow of electricity.

trade: A job that requires working with the hands or with machines.

vocational school: A school that prepares students for trade careers.

voltage: The force of an electric current.

INDEX

apprenticeships 14
business 17
circuit breaker 7, 8, 10
construction sites 19
electrical panel 7, 8, 19
electricity 4, 5, 7, 8, 11, 12, 20
electric shock 8, 12
insulated gloves 12
journeyworkers 17
license 17
light fixture 8, 10
master electrician 17
power 4, 7, 8
problem-solving 15
safety glasses 12
solar panels 18
streetlights 18
switches 5, 8, 10
tools 11
vocational school 14
voltage tester 8, 11
wires 5, 8, 10, 11, 15

TO LEARN MORE

Finding more information is as easy as 1, 2, 3.
❶ Go to www.factsurfer.com
❷ Enter "electrician" into the search box.
❸ Choose your book to see a list of websites.